NATIONAL
GEOGRAPHIC
KiDS

weird but true! 2

350 OUTRAGEOUS FACTS

NATIONAL GEOGRAPHIC

SCHOLASTIC INC.

A bottlenose dolphin has a bigger brain than a human.

Snow leopards can't

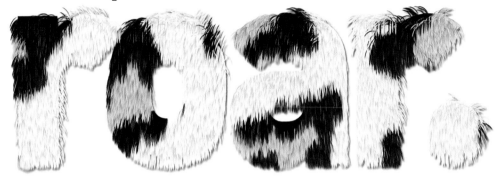

roar.

A BRITISH JEWELER MADE A **TEA BAG** DECORATED WITH **280** DIAMONDS—IT WAS WORTH **£7,500!** (ABOUT $12,000)

ONLY
FEMALE
BEES
STING.

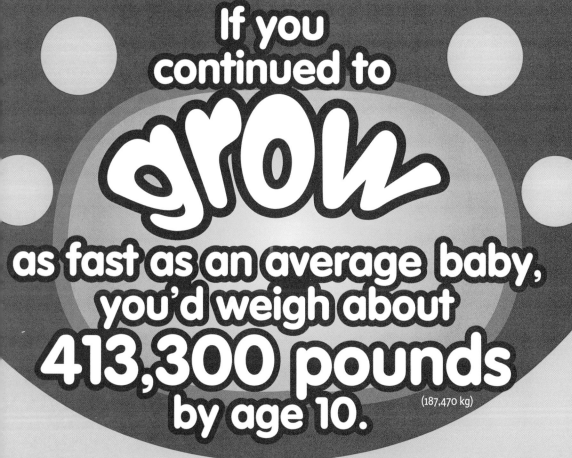

If you continued to **grow** as fast as an average baby, you'd weigh about **413,300 pounds** by age 10. (187,470 kg)

The average dream lasts about 20 minutes.

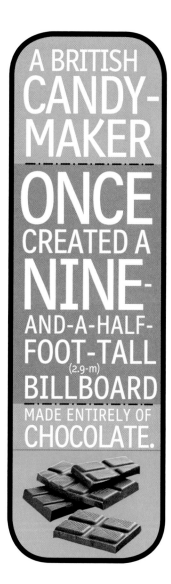

A BRITISH CANDY-MAKER ONCE CREATED A NINE-AND-A-HALF-FOOT-TALL (2.9-m) BILLBOARD MADE ENTIRELY OF CHOCOLATE.

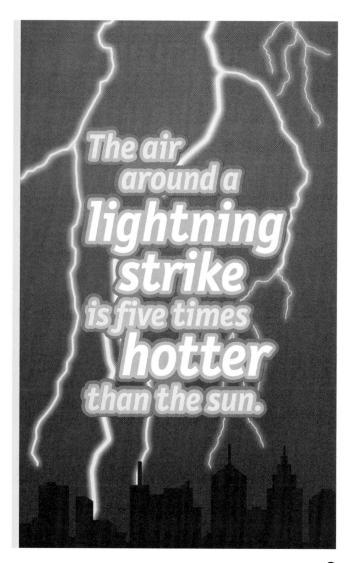

The air around a **lightning strike** is five times **hotter** than the sun.

9

Some **avalanches** travel more than

100

miles an hour.

(161 km/h)

A HUMAN BONE IS FIVE TIMES STRONGER THAN A PIECE OF STEEL OF THE SAME WEIGHT.

THE LONGEST RAW EGG TOSS WAS 150 YARDS. (137 m)

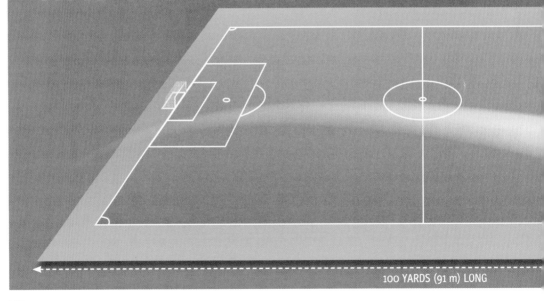

100 YARDS (91 m) LONG

THE DOTS ON DICE ARE CALLED PIPS.

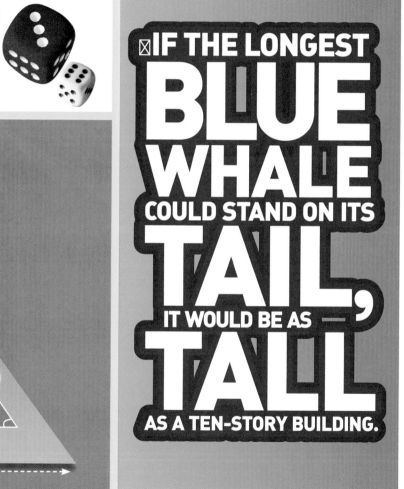

IF THE LONGEST **BLUE WHALE** COULD STAND ON ITS **TAIL,** IT WOULD BE AS **TALL** AS A TEN-STORY BUILDING.

13

Bats have thumbs.

ROCKETS MUST TRAVEL

AT LEAST
25,000 MILES AN HOUR
(40,234 km/h)
TO **ESCAPE EARTH'S GRAVITY.**

There have been at least
four major
ice ages.

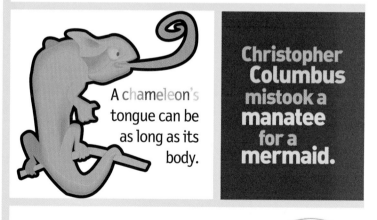

A chameleon's tongue can be as long as its body.

Christopher **Columbus** mistook a **manatee** for a **mermaid.**

Light travels *faster* than sound.

A newborn puppy can take up to **two months to start wagging** its tail.

Popcorn can pop up to three feet into the air.
(0.9 m)

The **London Bridge** that kept **falling down** is now in Arizona, in the United States.

A *ZEPTOSECOND* IS ONE-BILLIONTH OF A TRILLIONTH OF A SECOND.

NOTHING CAN ESCAPE FROM A BLACK HOLE.

AN AMERICAN MAN COOKED 427 OMELETS IN 30 MINUTES.

Some butterflies' **ears** are on their **wings.**

Fingernails grow faster than toenails.

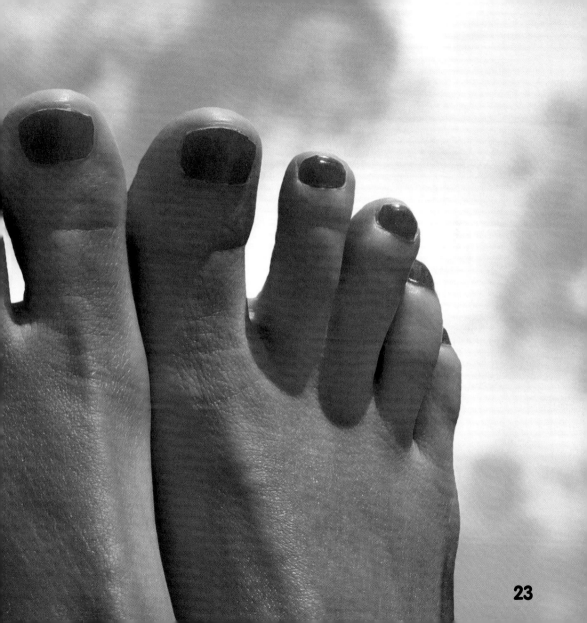

A camel can drink 500 cups (118 L) of water in ten minutes.

Gelotology is the study of laughter.

A supermarket in South Africa created a pizza that was 122 feet 8 inches across (37.4 m) and weighed as much as two male African elephants.

IF YOU TRAVELED AT THE SPEED OF LIGHT, YOU COULD REACH PLUTO IN JUST FOUR HOURS.

SOME FROGS GLOW WHEN THEY EAT FIREFLIES.

MEN GET THE HICCUPS MORE OFTEN THAN WOMEN DO.

A *JIFFY* is one-hundredth of a second.

THE WORLD'S TALLEST WATERFALL, CALLED ANGEL FALLS, IS TALLER THAN FIVE WASHINGTON MONUMENTS STACKED UP.

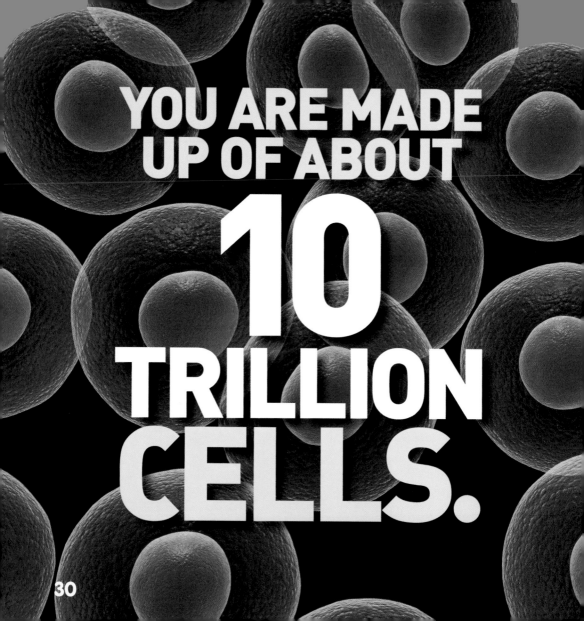

YOU ARE MADE UP OF ABOUT 10 TRILLION CELLS.

CHEWING GUM was banned in Singapore until 2004.

THE WORLD'S FIRST HANDHELD MOBILE PHONE COST $3,995.

The length of your arms stretched out is about equal to your height.

YOUR BRAIN IS SOMETIMES MORE ACTIVE WHEN YOU SLEEP THAN WHEN YOU'RE AWAKE.

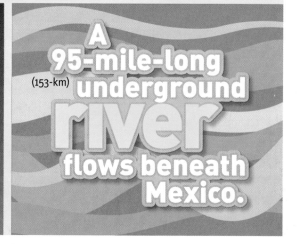

A 95-mile-long (153-km) underground river flows beneath Mexico.

Americans eat 1.2 billion pounds (544 million kg) of potato chips a year—more than ten times the weight of Egypt's Great Pyramid.

DINOSAUR **BONES** WERE MISTAKEN FOR **DRAGON BONES** WHEN THEY WERE DISCOVERED MORE THAN 2,000 YEARS AGO.

NEWBORN BABIES ARE COLOR-BLIND.

A 5,000-year-old piece of chewing gum was discovered in Finland.

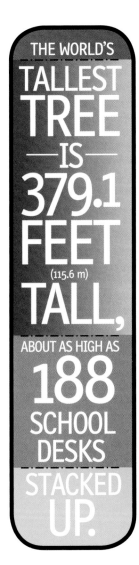

THE WORLD'S **TALLEST TREE** —IS— **379.1 FEET** (115.6 m) **TALL,** ABOUT AS HIGH AS **188 SCHOOL DESKS** STACKED UP.

A PIECE OF **CAKE** MORE THAN **4,000** YEARS OLD WAS FOUND IN A **TOMB** IN EGYPT.

MALE MOSQUITOES DON'T **BITE.**

One year on Neptune lasts about 165 Earth years.

ASTRONAUT **NEIL** ARMSTRONG LEFT HIS **SPACE BOOTS** ON THE **MOON.**

THE **FIRST** MICROWAVE **OVEN** WAS ALMOST AS **TALL** AS A REFRIGERATOR.

Some spiders eat their own webs.

There are about 16 million thunderstorms on Earth every year.

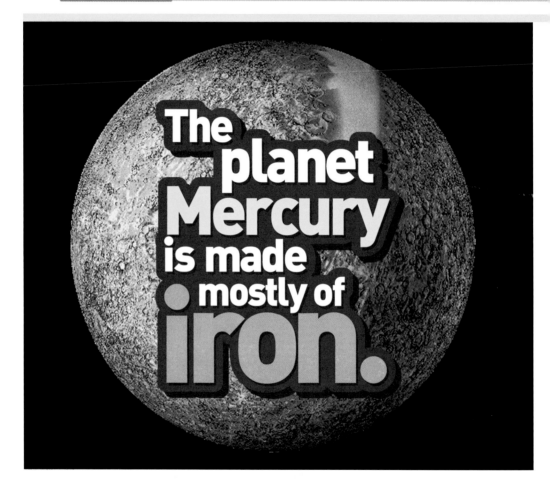

The planet Mercury is made mostly of iron.

About **61** percent of your body weight is water.

PANAMANIAN GOLDEN FROGS catch the attention of a mate by sitting on a riverbank and waving.

Until the mid-1800s, there was **NO DIFFERENCE BETWEEN LEFT AND RIGHT SHOES.**

The **ICEBERG** hit by the *TITANIC* is thought to have been about **100,000** years old.

A **METEORITE** SCULPTED TO LOOK LIKE A **CHICKEN SANDWICH** sold for **$20,000.**

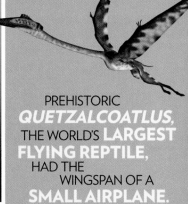

PREHISTORIC *QUETZALCOATLUS,* THE WORLD'S **LARGEST FLYING REPTILE,** HAD THE WINGSPAN OF A **SMALL AIRPLANE.**

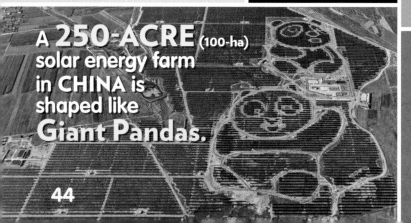

A **250-ACRE** (100-ha) solar energy farm in **CHINA** is shaped like **Giant Pandas.**

A RAT'S NOSTRILS SMELL independently of each other.

PENGUINS are attracted to the smell of **ROTTEN EGGS.**

BUS STOPS in KONAGAI, JAPAN, ARE SHAPED LIKE FRUIT.

HERMIT CRABS use their LARGE LEFT CLAW for defense and their SMALL RIGHT CLAW to collect and eat food.

That's Weird!

You can buy **GLOW-IN-THE-DARK DOUGHNUTS** at a BAKERY in AUSTRALIA.

HORSES can make more **FACIAL EXPRESSIONS** than **CHIMPS** and **DOGS.**

THE HEARTS
OF SOME
HUMMINGBIRDS
CAN BEAT MORE THAN

1,000

TIMES A MINUTE.

The ancient
Aztec used cacao
(cocoa) beans
as money.

Rhinoceroses don't sweat.

A hill in New Zealand is named
Taumatawhakatangihangakoauauo

IT'S POSSIBLE TO SMELL
SCENTS IN DREAMS.

tamateapokaiwhenuakitanatahu.

THE **GREAT BARRIER REEF** IN AUSTRALIA IS THE **BIGGEST LIVING STRUCTURE** ON EARTH.

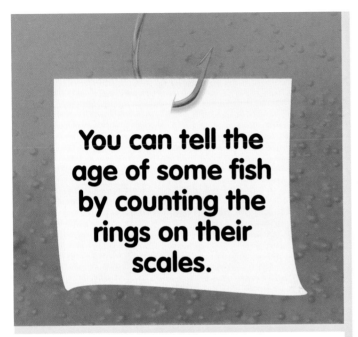

You can tell the age of some fish by counting the rings on their scales.

Bloodhounds can follow a scent that is **four** **days old.**

THE

SUN

IS

93

MILLION

MILES
AWAY.

(150 million km)

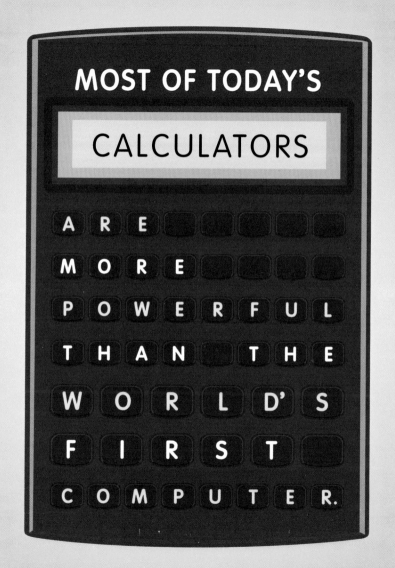

MOST OF TODAY'S

CALCULATORS

ARE MORE POWERFUL THAN THE WORLD'S FIRST COMPUTER.

ANIMALS THAT LAY EGGS DON'T HAVE BELLY BUTTONS.

A tiger's stripes are different on the left and right sides of its body.

The **first email was sent** in **1971.**

RUSSIA IS ONLY TWO MILES FROM ALASKA.
(3.2 km)

A GROUP OF BLUE JAYS IS CALLED A PARTY.

There are more than **250,000 different words** in the English language.

SHARKS HAVE NO BONES.

CATS CAN'T TASTE SWEETS.

Some robots can identify different cheeses.

56

A COCKROACH CAN LIVE FOR OVER A **WEEK** WITHOUT A HEAD.

Earth's core is about the same size as the planet Mars.

THE SAHARA DESERT IS LARGER THAN AUSTRALIA.

Venus is the **hottest planet** in our solar system.

LIONS SPEND ABOUT 20 HOURS A DAY RESTING.

A **TIGER** can eat more than **80 pounds** (36 kg) **of meat** in one sitting.

61

Most **people** spend about **five years** of their **lives** eating.

A HIPPO CAN RUN AS FAST AS **A HUMAN.**

A man **hiccuped** for 68 years straight.

METEORITES THE SIZE OF BASKETBALLS LAND ON EARTH ABOUT ONCE A MONTH.

NIGHTTIME RAINBOWS ARE CALLED MOONBOWS.

Enough whipped topping is manufactured every year to crisscross the United States more than 5 times.

63

75% of all animals are insects.

THE

WINGSPAN OF A

747

IS

LONGER

THAN THE

WRIGHT BROTHERS'

FIRST FLIGHT.

SCIENTISTS KNOW MORE ABOUT THE SURFACE OF **THE MOON** THAN **THE BOTTOM OF THE OCEAN.**

ON SUNNY DAYS, THE **EIFFEL TOWER** IN **PARIS, FRANCE, LEANS TOWARD THE SHADE.**

Engineers reversed the flow of the Chicago River.

Crocodiles can't chew.

65

A dog can make about

different facial expressions.

The Earth is slightly pear-shaped.

A zebra's skin is black; only its fur is striped.

A TROPICAL **ANT** CAN SNAP ITS JAWS TOGETHER AT A SPEED OF 145 MILES AN HOUR, (233 km/h) FASTER THAN ANY OTHER ANIMAL!

It takes the average 10-year-old kid

about 20 minutes to fall asleep.

MOUNT EVEREST GROWS MORE THAN ONE-EIGHTH OF AN INCH (3 mm) EACH YEAR.

1/8 inch

"Old man"

is a nickname for a male **kangaroo.**

One million seconds is 11 days, 13 hours, 46 minutes, and 40 seconds.

The brighter the star, the **shorter** its life span.

French fries came from

Belgium, not France.

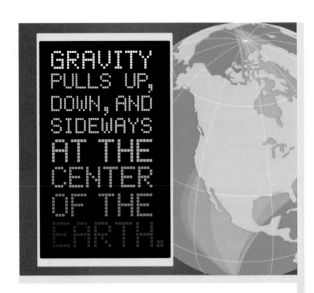

GRAVITY PULLS UP, DOWN, AND SIDEWAYS AT THE CENTER OF THE EARTH.

WHEN YOU SEE LIGHTNING, IT'S TRAVELING AT ABOUT

227 MILLION MILES AN HOUR.

(365 million km/h)

THERE ARE MORE TV SETS IN THE UNITED STATES THAN THERE ARE PEOPLE IN THE UNITED KINGDOM.

A **volcano** in Italy has been erupting for 2,000 years.

TURTLES LIVED ON EARTH BEFORE DINOSAURS DID.

Queen Margherita of Savoy ordered the first pizza delivery in 1889.

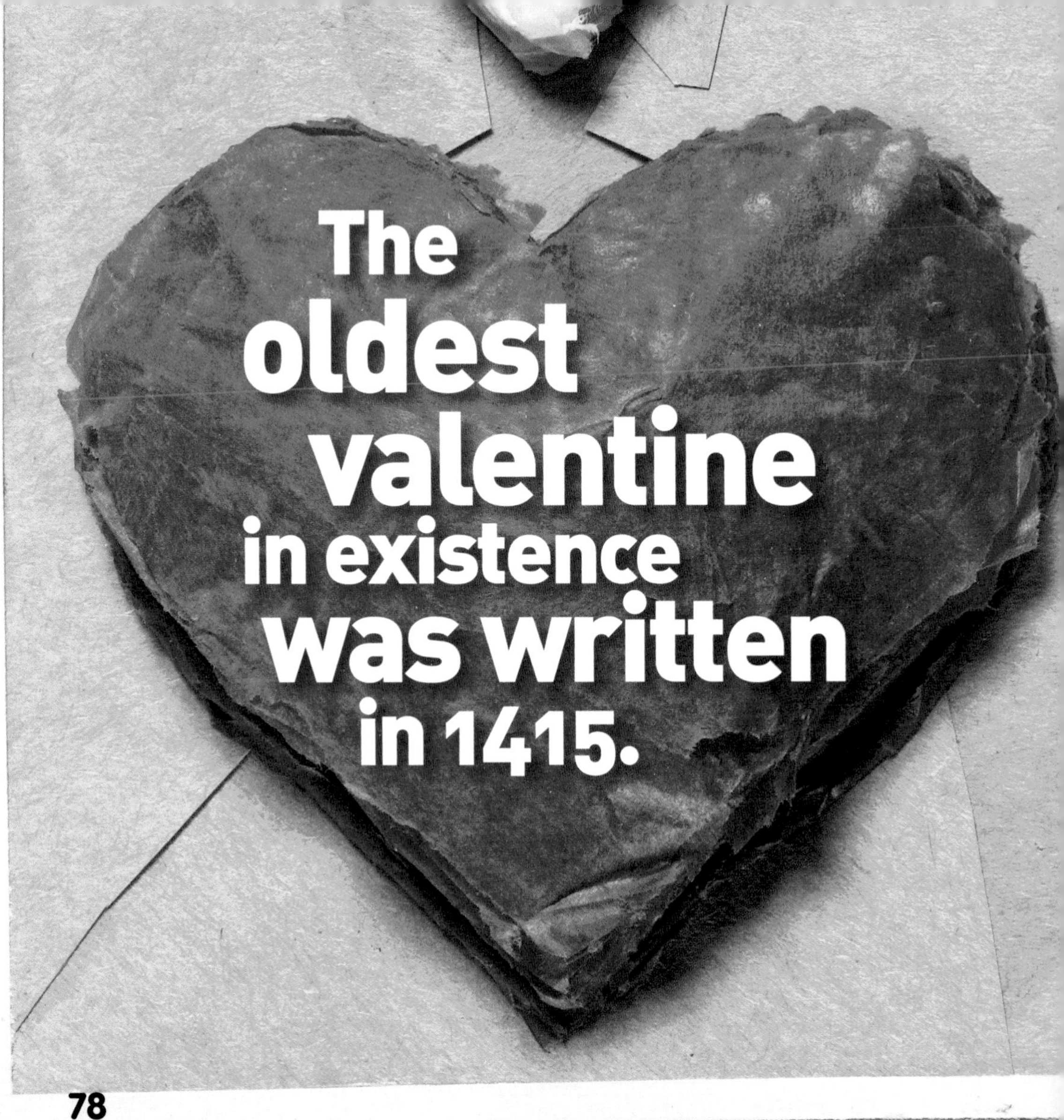

The
oldest
valentine
in existence
was written
in 1415.

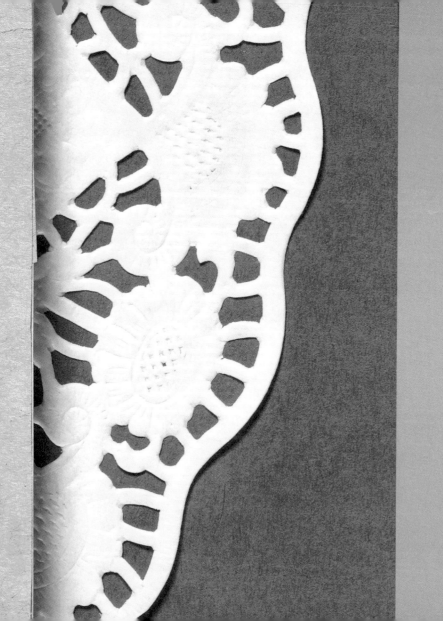

GIRAFFES WERE ONCE CALLED CAMELOPARDS BECAUSE PEOPLE THOUGHT THEY WERE HALF CAMEL ~AND~ HALF LEOPARD.

THERE IS NO SOUND IN SPACE.

Of any animal, the **pig** has a **diet** most like a human's.

Couples in Finland can **get married in a chapel built out of snow.**

Some chickens lay green or blue eggs.

You take about **25,000 breaths** every day.

The longest a person
has gone without
sleep
is ten days.

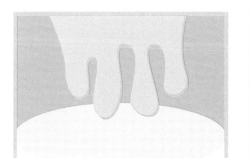

A DAIRY COW PRODUCES ABOUT 100,000 GLASSES OF MILK IN ITS LIFETIME.

Yo-yos rode on two space shuttles.

MEENAKSHI AMMAN, a Hindu temple in India, **CONTAINS AN ESTIMATED 33,000 SCULPTURES.**

YOU CAN LEARN PROFESSIONAL ACROBATIC and **CIRCUS ACTS** at a clown college in Illinois, U.S.A.

11 of the 12 ASTRONAUTS who walked on the moon had been **BOY SCOUTS.**

Archaeologists recently found a **3,700-YEAR-OLD CERAMIC JUG** with a **SMILEY FACE** painted on it.

WHEN THE DINOSAUR *Diplodocus* whipped its **45-foot** (13.7-m)- **long tail,** it may have **CAUSED a SONIC BOOM.**

During medieval times, **HAIR BALLS** were used as an **ANTIDOTE TO POISONS.**

The **Floating Instrument Platform (FLIP)** is designed to ROTATE A FULL 90 DEGREES in the ocean for underwater research.

In Spanish, *ARMADILLO* means **"LITTLE ARMORED ONE."**

For more than **100** years, the **IOWA STATE FAIR** has commissioned a **COW SCULPTURE** made from **600 POUNDS** of **BUTTER.** (272 kg)

There was once a **BEAVER POND** where **NEW YORK CITY'S TIMES SQUARE** currently stands.

FEMALE **MOUNTAIN GOATS** are called **NANNIES.**

That's Weird!

KOALAS STAY AWAKE FOR ONLY FOUR HOURS A DAY.

IT IS IMPOSSIBLE **TO SNEEZE** WITH YOUR **EYES OPEN.**

The **PRAYING MANTIS** is the only insect that can **LOOK OVER ITS SHOULDER.**

JUPITER HAS 63 MOONS.

Stretched out, your **digestive system** is nearly **30 feet long.**

(9.5 m)

Apples are one-quarter air.

THAT'S WEIRD!

Babies yawn before they are born.

Scents smell better through your

right nostril *than your left.*

A GROUP OF PORCUPINES IS CALLED A PRICKLE.

Eating shrimp can turn white flamingos pink.

KETCHUP was originally SOLD AS MEDICINE.

The average person **walks** about **80,000 miles** (128,750 km) in a lifetime.

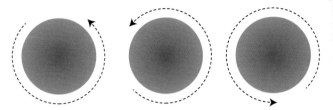

That's more than three times around the world!

The **NORTH POLE** is **warmer than the** SOUTH POLE.

CATERPILLARS have mouths, but **BUTTERFLIES** don't.

Earth is the only planet not named after a **Greek or Roman god.**

You can tell lions apart by the spots at the base of their whiskers.

Hippopotomonstros

Bees visit about five million flowers to make one average-size jar of honey.

esquippedaliophobia is the fear of long words.

Recycling one soda can a TV for three hours.

saves enough energy to run

Only **MALE TOADS**

Croak.

A man **flung a coin** more than ten feet using his **earlobe as a slingshot.** (3 m)

Your tongue grows new **taste buds** about every two weeks.

THE BAHAMAS ONCE HAD AN UNDERSEA POST OFFICE.

The world's **biggest frog** IS THE SIZE OF A **house cat.**

The total earthworm population in the United States weighs ten times more than the total human population.

A **porcupine** can have 30,000 quills.

One **ear of corn** has about **500** kernels.

GIRAFFES

are one of the only animals **born with horns.**

Wearing a hat on your head helps warm your feet.

All cats are born with blue eyes.

MONKEYS CAN GO **BALD** IN OLD AGE, JUST LIKE HUMANS CAN.

(2.7 million kg)
SIX MILLION POUNDS OF **SPACE DUST** SETTLE ON EARTH EVERY YEAR.

A **3,000-YEAR-OLD MUMMY** CAN STILL HAVE **FINGERPRINTS.**

A **snowflake** can take up to **two hours** to fall from a **cloud** to the ground.

PUMPKINS ALSO COME IN **RED, GREEN, YELLOW, BLUE, TAN & WHITE.**

Your skeleton

has about **300 BONES** when you are born, but only **206** by the time you grow up.

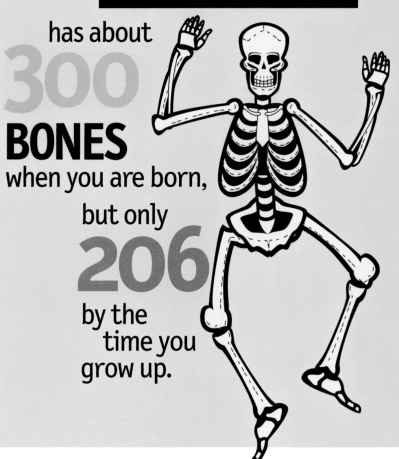

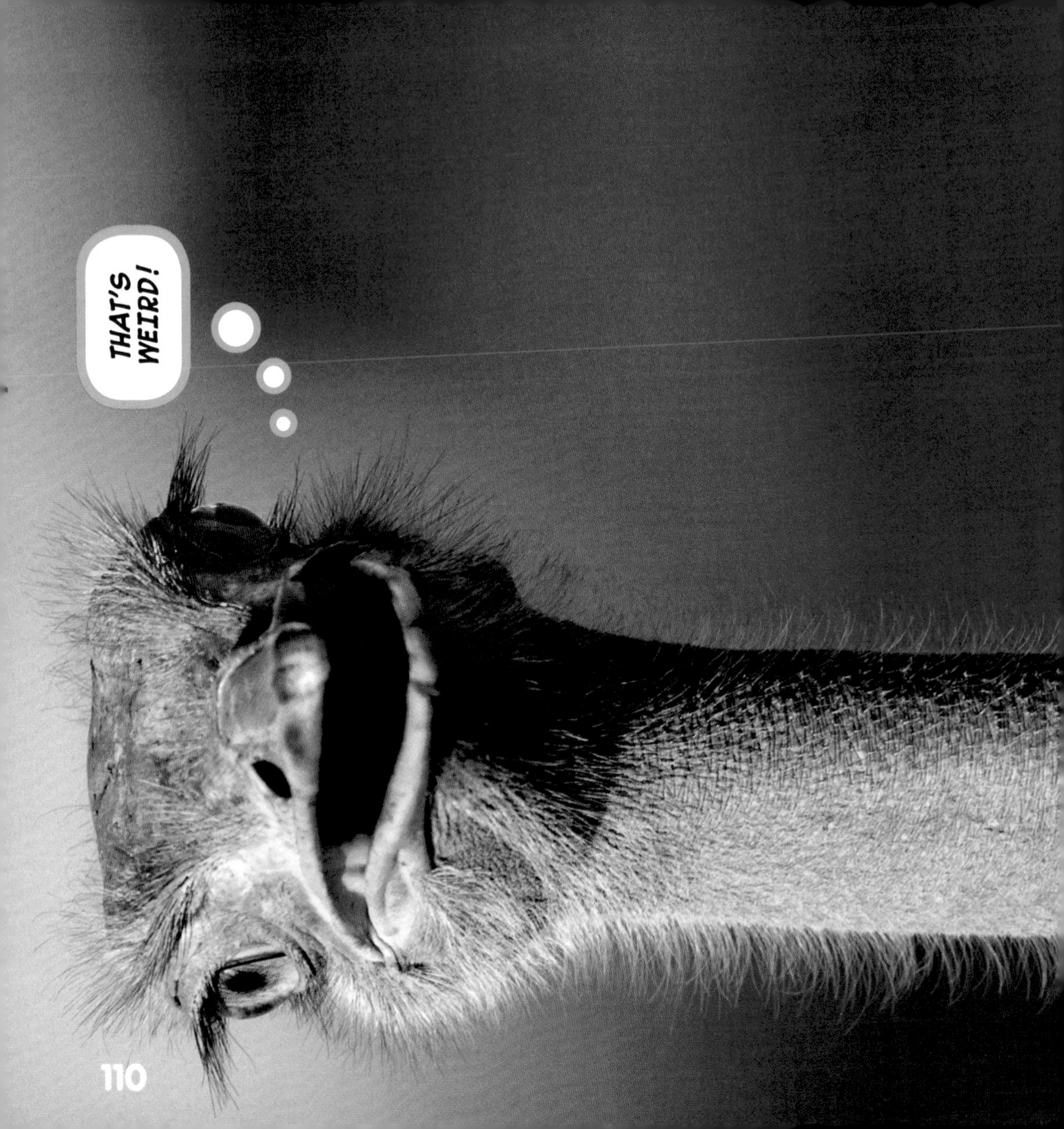
THAT'S WEIRD!

An ostrich's eye is bigger than its brain.

LINED UP END TO END, ALL THE

HARRY POTTER
BOOKS SOLD
COULD CIRCLE THE EARTH
MORE THAN
TWICE.

TARANTULAS CAN LIVE FOR UP TO **20** YEARS.

SOME OF THE FIRST SOLES ON
NIKE
SHOES
WERE MADE BY
POURING RUBBER
INTO A
WAFFLE IRON.

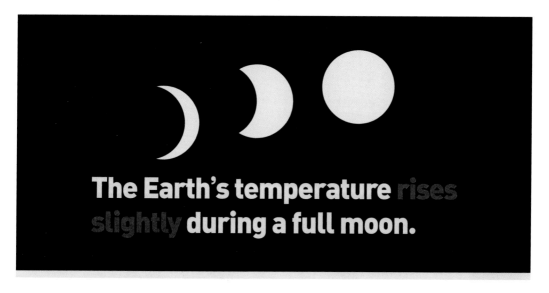

The Earth's temperature rises slightly **during a full moon.**

A Rubik's Cube can make
43,252,003,274,489,856,000
different **combinations.**

Popsicles

WERE INVENTED BY AN

11-year-old.

AN OSTRICH
CAN RUN AS FAST AS A
RACEHORSE.

Sharks have existed **LONGER** than trees.

ONE (5 mL) TEASPOON OF SEAWATER CONTAINS FIVE MILLION LIVING ORGANISMS.

From about **March 21** to September 23 the **sun never sets** at the **North Pole.**

SOME WORMS CAN GROW

Scientists found a **4,000–year-old "lunch box"** in the Bernese Alps.

Winter lasts for 21 years on Uranus.

TO 100 FEET LONG.
(31 m)

Most **squid** have three hearts.

ASTRONAUTS **GROW** — UP TO — 3 INCHES
(7.6 cm)
TALLER IN OUTER **SPACE.**

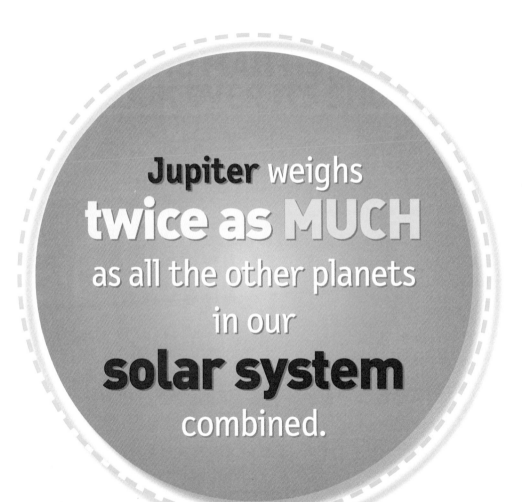

Jupiter weighs **twice as MUCH** as all the other planets in our **solar system** combined.

ABOUT

75

PERCENT

OF ALL

VOLCANOES

ARE

UNDERWATER.

A HIPPO'S LIPS ARE ABOUT TWO FEET WIDE.

(0.6 m)

GIGANTIC JETS = LIGHTNING THAT **SHOOTS UP FROM CLOUDS** INTO THE ATMOSPHERE INSTEAD OF **DOWN TO EARTH**

Professional tennis players **GRUNT** at a higher pitch **when they are LOSING A GAME** than when they are winning, a study found.

RAVENS roll around in the **SNOW.**

Tourists throw more than **one million DOLLARS** into **ROME, ITALY'S TREVI FOUNTAIN** every year.

DOCTORS RECENTLY FOUND **27** CONTACT LENSES LOST IN A **woman's eye.**

You can stay in a **CABIN** in the **SHAPE OF AN OWL** in southwest France.

The **PUPILS** of an ORIENTAL FIRE-BELLIED TOAD are shaped like **TRIANGLES.**

TORTOISES can **FEEL** when their **SHELLS ARE BEING TOUCHED.**

Some **SPIDERS** have ABDOMENS that look like **DISCO BALLS.**

A BAG USED TO COLLECT ROCKS ON THE MOON during the Apollo 11 mission **SOLD AT AN AUCTION** for $**1.8 MILLION.**

IN RUSSIA, it is considered **BAD LUCK** to **SHAKE HANDS** in the **THRESHOLD** of a **DOORWAY.**

Thieves in ENGLAND recently stole **88 POUNDS** (40 kg) of prize-winning **cheddar cheese.**

That's Weird!

FAIRY-WREN BIRDS teach their UNHATCHED CHICKS a **"PASSWORD"** to keep other birds from sneaking into the nest.

SOUTH AFRICA'S
GIANT BULLFROG
SOMETIMES ATTACKS LIONS.

If you weigh

50 pounds (23 kg) on Earth,

you would weigh about

3 pounds (1.4 kg) on Pluto.

ONLY **MALE** TURKEYS GOBBLE; **FEMALES CLICK.**

It would take about

788,832,000

two-inch yellow
(5-cm)
sticky notes
to encircle the globe.

OYSTERS
CHANGE
FROM
MALE
TO FEMALE.

A space **suit** costs about **ten** million dollars.

el**eph**a**n**ts

Without clothes, you would start to **feel cold** at **77°F.**

(25°C)

The world's first **underwater hotel** is in Key Largo, Florida, U.S.A.

can use their trunks as snorkels.

Fish can't close their eyes.

Detached
sea star
arms
sometimes grow
new >>>>
bodies.

Your eyes produce a teaspoon of tears every hour. (5 mL)

When you have lived for **2.4 billion seconds,** you will be **75 years old.**

Originally carrots were **purple,** not orange.

1,000,000,000,000,000 (that's one quadrillion) **ants** live on Earth.

8,962 people made snow **angels** at the **same** time on the grounds of the North Dakota State Capitol in the U.S.A.

The flag of every **country** in the world has at least one of the five colors in the Olympic **rings:** blue, yellow, **black,** green, **and red.**

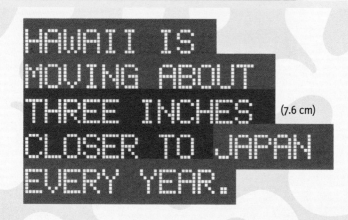

HAWAII IS MOVING ABOUT THREE INCHES CLOSER TO JAPAN EVERY YEAR.

(7.6 cm)

About
150,000 hairs
are growing on your head
right now.

Geckos ———
——— can *break off*
their own tails. ———

A litter of kittens is also called a kindle.

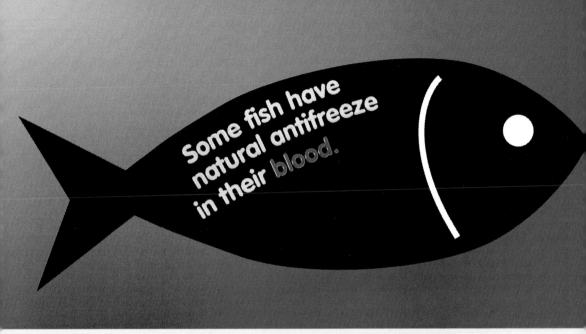

Some fish have natural antifreeze in their blood.

HUMANS AND SLUGS SHARE MORE THAN HALF OF THEIR GENES.

Alligators' eggs hatch male babies in hot temperatures and female babies in cooler temperatures.

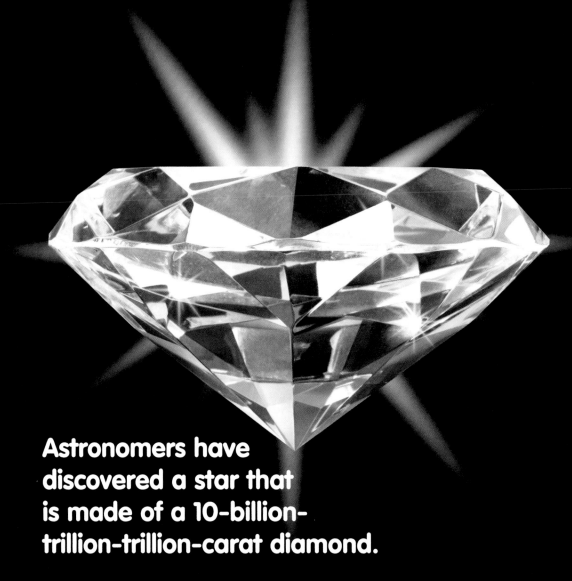

Astronomers have discovered a star that is made of a 10-billion-trillion-trillion-carat diamond.

A head of **broccoli** is made up of **hundreds of small flower buds.**

A storm
on Neptune was
as wide as ...

the entire
Earth.

Chewing **gum** can make your heart beat **faster.**

A 158-year-old **holiday card** was auctioned off in the U.K. for nearly **£22,250** (about $35,000).

The **surface** of the Atlantic Ocean is **saltier** than the surface of the **Pacific Ocean.**

The
50 tallest
mountains
in the world
are all in
Asia.

A dog's **nose print** is as unique as a **human fingerprint.**

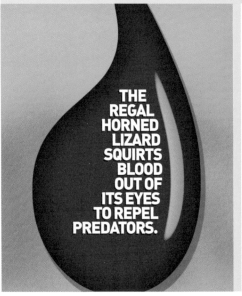

THE REGAL HORNED LIZARD SQUIRTS BLOOD OUT OF ITS EYES TO REPEL PREDATORS.

Your eyes can see about **TEN MILLION** different colors.

Didaskaleinophobia

is the fear of going to school.

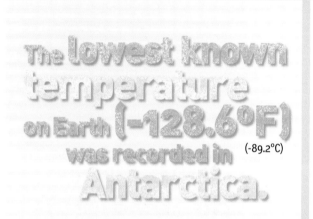

The **lowest known** temperature on Earth **(-128.6°F)** (-89.2°C) was recorded in **Antarctica.**

Ancient Egyptians took up to 70 days to make a mummy.

BEFORE TOOTHPASTE WAS INVENTED, SOME PEOPLE CLEANED THEIR TEETH WITH **CHARCOAL.**

The **Great Wall of China** spans roughly **4,500 miles—** (7,240 km) that's almost as long as the continent of **Africa.**

URP!

SHEEP BURPS CONTRIBUTE TO GLOBAL WARMING.

The heaviest known lobster weighed **44.6** (20.2 kg) **pounds.**

September begins on the same day of the week as **December every year.**

A WOMAN IN CALIFORNIA, U.S.A., REMEMBERS ALMOST EVERY DAY OF HER LIFE ...

SINCE SHE WAS 11.

Tyrannosaurus **rex** means "tyrant lizard king" in Latin.

GRRR!

The **sun** has enough **energy** to burn for **100 billion** more years.

A swordfish can swim ...

**about as fast as
a cheetah can run.**

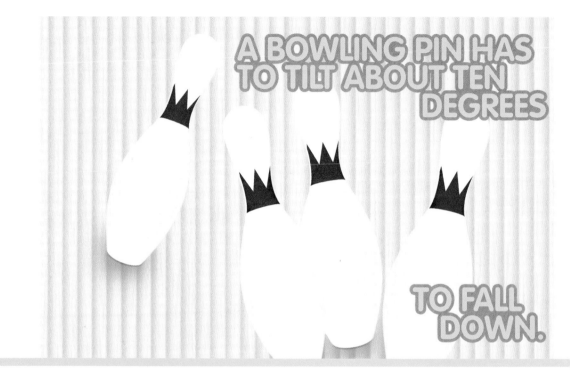

A BOWLING PIN HAS TO TILT ABOUT TEN DEGREES

TO FALL DOWN.

A PENNSYLVANIA BAKERY MADE A

The hottest stars are blue.

SCIENTISTS BELIEVE THAT SATURN'S RINGS WILL EVENTUALLY DISAPPEAR.

HOT DOG THAT WAS **54 FEET LONG.**
(16 m)

157

It would take a stack of **more than**

nine

Empire State Buildings to equal the average depth of the ocean.

The **"barking pigeon"** has a call that sounds like a **loud dog.**

SAND

melts at around 3000°F.

(1649°C)

ALL OF TODAY'S PET HAMSTERS CAN BE TRACED BACK TO **ONE HAMSTER FAMILY** THAT LIVED IN **SYRIA** IN 1930.

A HOUSE CAT'S TOP SPEED IS ABOUT

31 MILES AN HOUR.
(50 km/h)

The largest **spider** in the world is wider than a **basketball.**

An average of about **353,000** people are **born** every day.

The oldest bat fossil ever found was
50 million years old.

When **bald eagles** were named, the word **"bald"** meant **"white."**

There is real **GOLD** in the sun.

Humans **blink** about **17,000 times a day.**

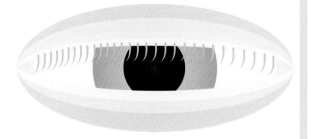

GLASS CAN LAST FOR MILLIONS OF YEARS ON EARTH.

THE LONGEST GAME OF MONOPOLY PLAYED IN A TREE HOUSE LASTED **286** HOURS.

Some **giant jellyfish** have **tentacles** that could **stretch** more than the length of a basketball **court.**

A **toucan's SONG** resembles **croaking frogs.**

The **BRAIN WAVES** between two people **SYNC** when they are in conversation.

Groups of **SPERM WHALES** sometimes **SLEEP VERTICALLY** (straight up and down).

A **SUBWAY CAR** in Taipei City, Taiwan, was recently **DECORATED** to look like a **SWIMMING POOL.**

The Mars rover **CURIOSITY** played the song **"HAPPY BIRTHDAY TO YOU"** to mark the first anniversary of its landing.

The **BIBLIO-MAT** is a VENDING MACHINE in Toronto, Canada, that **DISPENSES BOOKS.**

Some **CATERPILLARS** live in tunnels inside leaves.

A woman won **$10,000** for a **WEDDING DRESS** she made out of toilet paper.

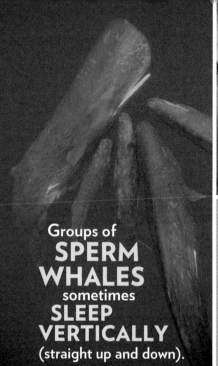

A study found that **HEAT** makes **PEOPLE MEANER.**

The average **AMERICAN** eats **45 PINTS** (21 L) of **ICE CREAM PER YEAR.**

BEES are more likely to land on a painting that **features FLOWERS** than **still-life** paintings, researchers found.

SCIENTISTS have created **ONIONS THAT DON'T MAKE YOU CRY** when cutting them.

BABIES can recognize the **DIFFERENCE** between **LANGUAGES** before they're **BORN.**

BABY HEDGEHOGS are called **HOGLETS.**

That's Weird!

About 12,000 animal crackers are created every minute.

About one-tenth of the Earth's surface is covered in ice.

Houseflies buzz in

A QUICK-HANDED **PERFORMER TWISTED 747** BALLOON SCULPTURES IN **1** HOUR.

the key of F.

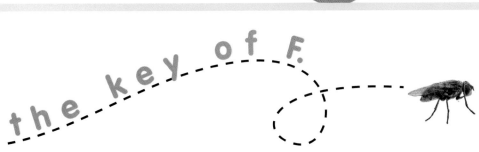

The **air** trapped inside an **iceberg** can be **thousands of years old.**

To reach the top of the Leaning Tower of Pisa, you have to climb a 293-step spiral staircase.

Chickens
see daylight
45 minutes
before humans do.

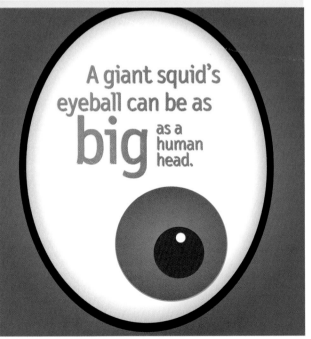

A giant squid's eyeball can be as **big** as a human head.

There's a **one in a** **trillion** chance that a piece of **space** **junk** will land on your **house** **today.**

YOU COULD ONCE **CALL HOME** FROM AN **ICE** TELEPHONE BOOTH AT A FESTIVAL IN **ALASKA,** U.S.A.

THE WORLD'S TINIEST SEAHORSE IS SMALLER THAN A POSTAGE STAMP.

THE LARGEST **HURRICANES** CAN MEASURE **TEN MILES** (16 km) **FROM TOP TO BOTTOM.**

The largest salamanders can grow as long as bicycles.

174

A Canadian juice company made a 195-gallon (738-L) fruit smoothie that could have filled four bathtubs.

Apes laugh when tickled.

If you spent a **dollar** every second, it would take about **32 years** to spend a **billion dollars.**

DOLPHINS SLEEP WITH ONE EYE **OPEN.**

An octopus can have nearly **2,000 suckers** on its arms.

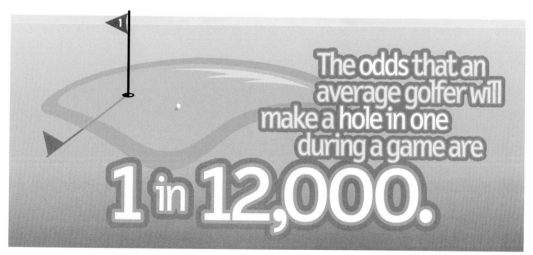

The odds that an average golfer will make a hole in one during a game are **1 in 12,000.**

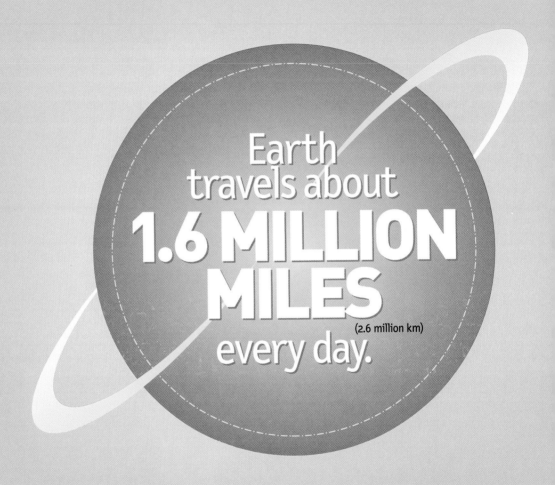

Earth travels about **1.6 MILLION MILES** (2.6 million km) every day.

AN ALLIGATOR GROWS ABOUT **3,000 TEETH** IN A LIFETIME.

MANATEES ARE RELATED TO **ELEPHANTS.**

A 14-pound (6.4-kg) pearl was found in a giant clam.

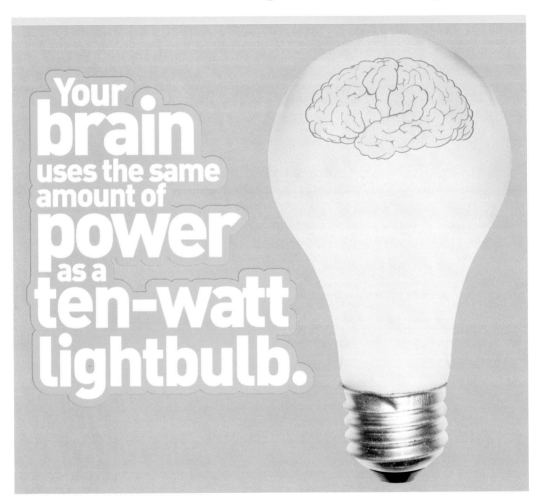

Your **brain** uses the same amount of **power** as a **ten-watt lightbulb.**

THERE ARE MORE TEXT MESSAGES SENT EACH DAY THAN THERE ARE PEOPLE ON EARTH.

A cornflake shaped like the U.S. state of Illinois sold for **$1,350.**

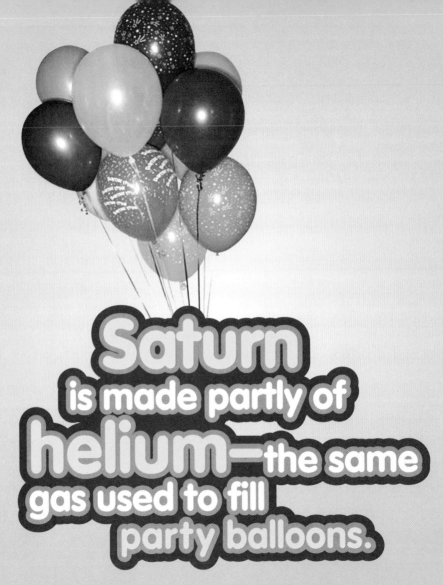

Saturn is made partly of **helium**—the same gas used to fill party balloons.

Most pirates never buried their loot.

A gold nugget found in California, U.S.A., weighed a whopping 160 pounds—about as much as 12 bowling balls.

(72.6 kg)

Kangaroos lick their forearms to stay cool.

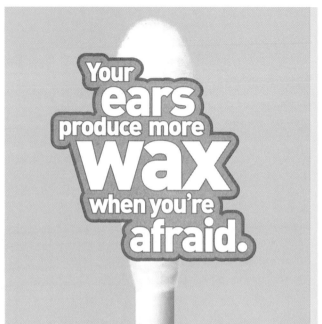

Your **ears** produce more **wax** when you're **afraid.**

YOUR **HEARTBEAT** IS SO POWERFUL THAT IT COULD **SHOOT WATER** SIX FEET (1.8 m) INTO THE AIR.

Nomads created **ice skates** made of **bone** at least **4,000 years ago.**

The **Queen** of **England** has a **crown studded** with more than **3,000** precious gems.

A **Tyrannosaurus rex** fossil was sold to a museum for more than **eight million** dollars.

The **binturong,** a southeast Asian mammal, smells like **buttered popcorn** when excited.

A cave in Croatia has a 1,683-foot-deep pit—the (513-m) **deepest hole on Earth.**

A snake can **eat prey** that is **twice the width** of its head.

A group of **sea otters** is called a raft.

The offspring of a whale and a dolphin is a **wholphin.**

650 HOUSE-FLIES

weigh less than

ONE OUNCE.
(28 g)

A rattlesnake's **rattle** is made of the same material as your fingernails.

195

A mouse's heart is shorter than a Tic Tac.

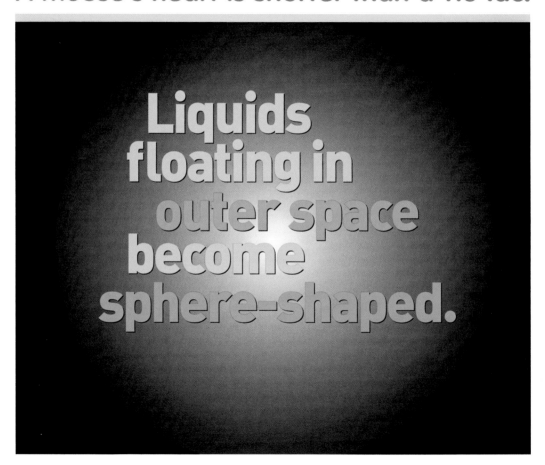

Liquids floating in outer space become sphere-shaped.

A seahorse can move its eyes in opposite directions.

A HUMAN EYELASH LASTS APPROXIMATELY THREE TO FIVE MONTHS.

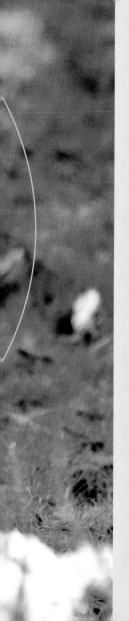

An **eagle** can spot a rabbit from more than a **mile** (1.6 km) **away.**

Forest fires can travel faster uphill than downhill.

Mice can have up to 105 babies a year.

MORE THAN TWO MILLION ANIMALS

A **sandcastle** in Maine, U.S.A., stood as **high** as a three-story building.

FLY IN AIRPLANES EVERY YEAR.

Peaches and almonds are related.

A **56**-LEAF CLOVER WAS DISCOVERED IN **JAPAN**.

A **red flag** was a symbol for **battle** in ancient **Rome.**

A **newborn koala** is about the size of a **jelly bean.**

THE WORD "PURPLE" COMES FROM A GREEK WORD FOR A TYPE OF SHELLFISH.

205

The highest known **jump** by a **pig** is 27.5 inches— (69.9 cm) that's the height of a St. Bernard!

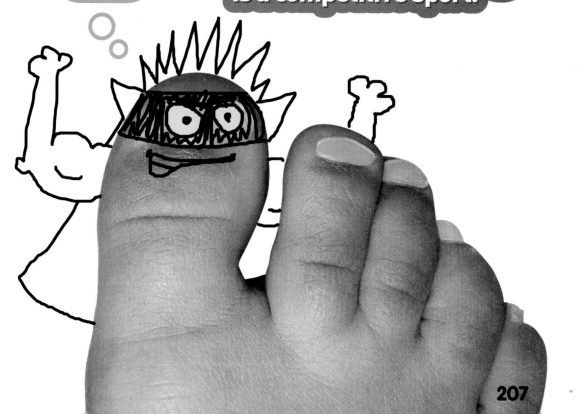

FACTFINDER

Boldface indicates illustrations.

FACTFINDER

PHOTOCREDITS

ISBN 978-1-338-71985-7

The publisher does not have any control over and does not assume any responsibility for author or third-party websites or their content.

12 11 10 9 8 7 6 5 4 3 2 1   20 21 22 23 24 25

Printed in the U.S.A.   40

First Scholastic printing, September 2020

Book designed by Rachel Hamm Plett, Moduza Design

The publisher would like to thank Jen Agresta, project manager; Sharon Thompson, researcher; Kelsey Turek, researcher; Michelle Harris, researcher; Robin Terry, project editor; Paige Towler, project editor; Eva Absher-Schantz, art director; Julide Dengel, art director; Kathryn Robbins, art director; Ruthie Thompson, designer; Lori Epstein, photo director; Jay Sumner, photo editor; Hillary Leo, photo editor; Alix Inchausti, production editor; and Anne LeongSon and Gus Tello, production assistants.